Poems Of Francis Scott Fitzgerald, A Classic Collection Book

Edited by
Debbie Brewer

Cover Portrait by
Gordon Bryant (1921)

ISBN-13: 978-0-244-85181-1

First Edition

Poems of Jane Austen

Poems of George Eliot

Poems of Anne Bronte

Poems of Charlotte Bronte

Poems of Emily Bronte

Poems of Charles Dickens

Poems of Mark Twain

Sonnets of Shakespeare

And more

*A
Classic
Collection
Book*

Poems Of
Francis Scott
Fitzgerald

Foreword

Francis Scott Fitzgerald (1896 – 1940) was a successful American novelist.

He was famous for four novels; 'This Side Of Paradise', 'The Beautiful And Damned', 'The Great Gatsby', and 'Tender Is The Night', which earned him recognition as one of the greatest American writers of the 20th century.

Less well known, but of equal importance, are his poems, which display his remarkable ability for descriptive and emotive poetry.

Poems by Francis Scott Fitzgerald:

- The Staying Up All Night
- Lamp In A Window
- Football
- Clay Feet
- Thousand And First Ship
- Rain Before Dawn
- My First Love
- On A Play Twice Seen
- Fragment
- A Poem Amory Sent To Eleanor And Which He Called "Summer Storm"
- A Poem That Eleanor Sent Amory Several Years Later
- Sleep Of A University
- Sad Catastrophe
- Princeton – The Last Day
- Oh Misseldine's
- We Leave Tonight

The Staying Up All Night

The warm fire.
The comfortable chairs.
The merry companions.
The stroke of twelve.
The wild suggestion.
The good sports.
The man who hasn't slept for
weeks.
The people who have done it
before.
The long anecdotes.
The best looking girl yawns.
The forced raillery.
The stroke of one.
The best looking girl goes to
bed.
The stroke of two.
The empty pantry.
The lack of firewood.
The second best looking girl

goes to bed.
The weather-beaten ones who
don't.
The stroke of four.
The dozing off.
The amateur 'life of the party.'

Lamp In A Window

Do you remember, before
keys turned in the locks,
When life was a close-up,
and not an occasional
letter,
That I hated to swim naked
from the rocks
While you liked absolutely
nothing better?

Do you remember many
hotel bureaus that had
Only three drawers? But the
only bother
Was that each of us got
holy, then got mad
Trying to give the third one
to the other.

East, west, the little car
turned, often wrong
Up an erroneous Alp, an
unmapped Savoy river.
We blamed each other, wild
were our words and strong,
And, in an hour, laughed
and called it liver.

And, though the end was
desolate and unkind:
To turn the calendar at June
and find December
On the next leaf; still,
stupid-got with grief, I find
These are the only quarrels
that I can remember.

Football

Now they're ready, now they're
waiting,
Now he's going to place the
ball.
There, you hear the referee's
whistle,
As of old the baton's fall.
See him crouching. Yes, he's got
it;
Now he's off around the end.
Will the interference save him?
Will the charging line now
bend?
Good he'free; no, see that
halfback
Gaining up behind him slow.
Crash! they're down; he threw
him nicely,—
Classy tackle, hard and low.
Watch that line, now crouching

waiting,
In their jerseys white and black;
Now they're off and charging,
making
Passage for the plunging back.
Buck your fiercest, run your
fastest,
Let the straight arm do the rest.
Oh, they got him; never mind,
though,
He could only do his best.
What is this? A new formation.
Look! their end acts like an ass.
See, he's beckoning for
assistance,
Maybe it's a forward pass.
Yes, the ball is shot to fullback,
He, as calmly as you please,
Gets it, throws it to the end; he
Pulls the pigskin down with
ease.
Now they've got him. No, they
haven't.

See him straight-arm all those
fools.
Look, he's clear. Oh, gee! don't
stumble.
Faster, faster, for the school.
There's the goal, now right
before you,
Ten yards, five yards, bless your
name!
Oh! you Newman, 1911,
You know how to play the
game.

Clay Feet

Clear in the morning I can
see them sometimes:
Men, gods and ghosts, slim
girls and graces—
Then the light grows, noon
burns, and soon there come
times
When I see but the pale and
ravaged places
Their glory long ago
adorned.—And seeing
My whole soul falters as an
invalid
Too often cheered. Did
something in their being
Of worth go from them
when my ideal did?

Men, gods and ghosts, cast
down by that young
damning,
You have no answer; I but
heard you say,
"Why, we are weak. We
failed a bit in shamming."
—So I am free! Will freedom
always weigh
So much around my heart?
For your defection,
Break! You who had me in
your keeping, break! Fall
From that great height to
this great imperfection!
Yet I must weep.—Yet can I
hate you all?

Thousand And First Ship

In the fall of sixteen
In the cool of the afternoon
I saw Helena
Under a white moon—
I heard Helena
In a haunted doze
Say: "I know a gay place
Nobody knows."

Her voice promised
She'd live with me there
She'd bring me everything—
I needn't care:
Patches to mend my clothes
When they were torn
Sunshine from Maryland,
Where I was born.

My kind of weather,
As wild as wild,
And a funny book
I wanted as a child;
Sugar and, you know,
Reason and rhyme,
And water like water
I had one time.

There'd be an orchestra
Bingo! Bango!
Playing for us
To dance the tango,
And people would clap
When we arose,
At her sweet face
And my new clothes

But more than all this
Was the promise she made
That nothing, nothing,
Ever would fade—
Nothing would fade
Winter or fall,
Nothing would fade,
Practically nothing at all.

Helena went off
And married another,
She may be dead
Or some man's mother.
I have no grief left
But I'd like to know
If she took him
Where she promised we'd go.

Rain Before Dawn

THE dull, faint patter in the
drooping hours
Drifts in upon my sleep and fills
my hair
With damp; the burden of the
heavy air
Is strewn upon me where my
tired soul cowers,
Shrinking like some lone queen
in empty towers
Dying. Blind with unrest I grow
aware:
The pounding of broad wings
drifts down the stair
And sates me like the heavy
scent of flowers.

I lie upon my heart. My eyes like hands
Grip at the soggy pillow. Now the dawn
Tears from her wetted breast the splattered blouse
Of night; lead-eyed and moist she straggles o'er the lawn,
Between the curtains brooding stares and stands
Like some drenched swimmer —
Death's within the house!

My First Love

All my ways she wove of light
Wove them half alive,
Made them warm and beauty-
bright...
So the shining, ambient air
Clothes the golden waters
where
The pearl fishers dive.

When she wept and begged a
kiss
Very close I'd hold her,
Oh I know so well in this
Fine, fierce joy of memory
She was very young like me
Tho' half an aeon older.

Once she kissed me very long,
Tip-toes out the door,
Left me, took her light along,
Faded as a music fades...
Then I saw the changing shades,
Colour-blind no more.

On A Play Twice Seen

HERE in the figured dark I watch
once more;
There with the curtain rolls a
year away,
A year of years — There was an
idle day
Of ours, when happy endings
didn't bore
Our unfermented souls, and
rocks held ore:
Your little face beside me, wide-
eyed, gay,
Smiled its own repertoire, while
the poor play
Reached me as a faint ripple
reaches shore.

Yawning and wondering an
evening through
I watch alone — and chatterings
of course
Spoil the one scene which
somehow did have charms;
You wept a bit, and I grew sad
for you
Right there, where Mr. X
defends divorce
And What's-Her-Name falls
fainting in his arms

Fragment

Every time I blow my nose I
think of you

And the mellow noise it makes

Says I'll be true –

With beers and wines

With Gertrude Steins,

Will all of that

I'm through –

'Cause every time I blow my no-
o-ose

I – think – of - you

A Poem Amory Sent To Eleanor And Which He Called "Summer Storm"

FAINT winds, and a song fading
and leaves falling,
Faint winds, and far away a
fading laughter . . .
And the rain and over the fields
a voice calling . . .

One grey blown cloud scurries
and lifts above,
Slides on the sun and flutters
there to waft her
Sisters on. The shadow of a
dove
Falls on the cote, the trees are
filled with wings;
And down the valley through
the crying trees
The body of the darker storm
flies; brings
With its new air the breath of
sunken seas
And slender tenuous thunder . .

.

But I wait . . .
Wait for the mists and for the
blacker rain—
Heavier winds that stir the veil
of fate,
Happier winds that pile her
hair;
Again
They tear me, teach me, strew
the heavy air
Upon me, winds that I know,
and storm.

There was a summer every rain
was rare;
There was a season every wind
was warm . . .
And now you pass me in the
mist . . . your hair
Rain-blown about you, damp
lips curved once more
In that wild irony, that gay
despair
That made you old when we
have met before;
Wraith-like you drift on out
before the rain,
Across the fields, blown with the
stemless flowers,
With your old hopes, dead
leaves and loves again—
Dim as a dream and wan with all
old hours
(Whispers will creep into the
growing dark . . .

Tumult will die over the trees)
Now night
Tears from her wetted breast
the splattered blouse
Of day, glides down the
dreaming hills, tear-bright,
To cover with her hair the eerie
green . . .
Love for the dusk . . . Love for
the glistening after;
Quiet the trees to their last tops
. . . serene . . .

Faint winds, and far away a
fading laughter . . .

A Poem That Eleanor Sent Amory Several Years Later

HERE, Earth-born, over the lilt of
the water,
Lisping its music and bearing a
burden of light,
Blossoming day as a laughing
and radiant daughter . . .
Here we may whisper unheard,
unafraid of the night.
Walking alone . . . was is
splendour, or what, we were
bound with,
Deep in the time when summer
lets down her hair?
Shadows we loved and the
patterns they covered the
ground with
Tapestries, mystical, faint in the
breathless air.

That was the day . . . and the
night for another story,
Pale as a dream and shadowed
with penciled trees—
Ghosts of the stars came by who
had sought for glory,
Whispered to us of peace in the
plaintive breeze,
Whispered of old dead faiths
that the day had shattered,
Youth the penny that bought
delight of the moon;
That was the urge that we knew
and the language that mattered
That was the debt that was paid
to the userer June.

Here, deepest of dreams, by the
waters that bring not
Anything back of the past that
we need not know,
What if the light is but sun and
the little streams sing not,
We are together, it seems . . . I
have loved you so . . .
What did the last night hold,
with the summer over,
Drawing us back to the home in
the changing glade?
What leered out of the dark in
the ghostly clover?
God! . . . till you stirred in your
sleep . . . and were wild afraid . .
.

Well . . . we have passed . . . we
are chronicle now to the eerie.
Curious metal from meteors
that failed in the sky;
Earth-born the tireless is
stretched by the water, quite
weary,
Close to this ununderstandable
changeling that's I . . .
Fear is an echo we traced to
Security's daughter;
Now we are faces and voices . . .
and less, too soon,
Whispering half-love over the
lilt of the water . . .
Youth the penny that bought
delight of the moon.

Sleep Of A University

WATCHING through the long,
dim hours
Like statued Mithras, stand
ironic towers;
Their haughty lines severe by
light
Are softened and gain tragedy
at night.
Self-conscious, cynics of their
charge,
Proudly they challenge the
dreamless world at large.

From pseudo-ancient Nassau
Hall, the bell
Crashes the hour, as if to
pretend 'All's well!'
Over the campus then the
listless breeze
Floats along drowsily, filtering
through the trees,
Whose twisted branches seem
to lie
Like point d'Alençon lace against
the sky
Of soft grey-black — a gorgeous
robe
Buttoned with stars, hung over
a tiny globe.

With life far-off, peace sits
supreme:
The college slumbers in a
fatuous dream,
While, watching through the
moonless hours
Like statued Mithras, stand the
ironic towers.

Sad Catastrophe

We don't want visitors, we said:
They come and sit for hours;
They come when we have gone
to bed;
They are imprisoned here by
showers;
They come when they are low
and bored–
Drink from the bottle of your
heart.
Once it is emptied, the gay
horde,
Shouting the Rubaiyat, depart.
I balked: I was at work, I cried;
Appeared unshaven or not at
all;

Was out of gin: the cook had died
Of small-pox–and more tales as tall.
On boor and friend I turned the same
Dull eye, the same impatient tone–
The ones with beauty, sense and fame
Perceived we wished to be alone.

But dull folk, dreary ones and
rude–
Long talker, lonely soul and
quack–
Who hereto hadn't dare
intrude,
Found us alone, swarmed to
attack,
Thought silence was attention;
rage
An echo of their own home's
war–
Glad we had ceased to "be
upstage."
–But the nice people came no
more.

Princeton – The Last Day

THE last light wanes and drifts
across the land,
The low, long land, the sunny
land of spires.
The ghosts of evening tune
again their lyres
And wander singing, in a
plaintive band
Down the long corridors of
trees. Pale fires
Echo the night from tower top
to tower.
Oh sleep that dreams and
dream that never tires,
Press from the petals of the
lotus-flower
Something of this to keep, the
essence of an hour!

No more to wait the twilight of

the moon
In this sequestrated vale of star
and spire;
For one, eternal morning of
desire
Passes to time and earthy
afternoon.
Here, Heracletus, did you build
of fire
And changing stuffs your
prophecy far hurled
Down the dead years; this
midnight I aspire
To see, mirrored among the
embers, curled
In flame, the splendour and the
sadness of the world.

Oh Misseldine's

Oh Misseldine's,
Dear Misseldine's
A dive we'll ne'er forget
The taste of its
banana splits
Is on our tonsils yet.

Its chocolate fudge
Makes livers budge
It's really too divine
And as we reel
We'll give one squeal
For dear old Misseldine's

We Leave Tonight

WE leave tonight . . .
Silent, we filled the still,
deserted street,
A column of dim grey,
And ghosts rose startled at the
muffled beat
Along the moonless way;
The shadowy shipyards echoed
to the feet
That turned from night and day.

And so we linger on the
windless decks,
See on the spectre shore
Shades of a thousand days, poor
grey-ribbed wrecks . . .
Oh, shall we then deplore
Those futile years!

See how the sea is white!
The clouds have broken and the
heavens burn
To hollow highways, paved with
gravelled light
The churning of the waves
about the stern
Rises to one voluminous
nocturne,
. . . We leave tonight.

For A Long Illness

Where did we store the
summer of our love?
Come here and help me find
it.
Search as I may there is no
trove,
Only a dusty last year's
calendar.
Without your breath in my
ear,
Your light in my eye to blind
it,
I cannot see in the dark.
Oh, tender
Was your touch in spring,
your barefoot voice—
In August we should find
graver music and rejoice.

A long Provence of time we
saw
For the end—to march
together
Through the white dust.
The wines are raw—
Still that we will drink
In the groves by the old
walls in the old weather.
Two who were hurt in the
first dawn
Of battle; first to be whole
again (let's think)
If the wars grow faint,
sweep over...
Come, we will rest in the
shade of the Invalides, the
lawn
Where there is luck only in
three-leaf clover.

Oh, Sister, Can You Spare Your Heart?

I may be a What-ho, a No-
can-do
Even a banker, but I can
love you
As well as a better man
a letter-man of fame
As well as any Mr. Whosis
you can name

The little break in my voice
—or Rolls-Royce
take your choice
I may lose
You must choose
So choose

A hundred thousand in gold
and you're sold
to the old
and I'm broke
when our days
are gold
I'm begging
begging
Oh, Sister, can you spare
your heart?

Those wealthy goats
In racoon coats
can wolf you away from me
But draw your latch
For an honest patch
the skin of necessity

(we'll make it a tent, dear)

The funny patch in my
pants
take a chance
ask your aunts
What's a loss
You must toss
So toss!

A gap inside that's for good.
You'll be good
As you should
Touch wood!
I'm begging
begging
Oh, Sister, can you spare
your heart?

Marching Streets

Death slays the moon and the
long dark deepens,
Hastens to the city, to the drear
stone-heaps,
Films all eyes and whispers on
the corners,
Whispers to the corners that the
last soul sleeps.

Gay grow the streets now
torched by yellow lamplight,
March all directions with a long
sure tread.
East, west they wander through
the blinded city,
Rattle on the windows like the
wan-faced dead.

Ears full of throbbing, a babe
awakens startled,
Sends a tiny whimper to the still
gaunt room.
Arms of the mother tighten
round it gently,
Deaf to the patter in the far-
flung gloom.

Old streets hoary with dear,
dead foot-steps
Loud with the tumbrils of a gold
old age
Young streets sand-white still
un-heeled and soulless,
Virgin with the pallor of the
fresh-cut page.

Black streets and alleys, evil girl
and tearless,
Creeping leaden footed each in
thin, torn coat,
Wine-stained and miry, mire
choked and winding,
Wind like choking fingers on a
white, full throat.

White lanes and pink lanes,
strung with purpled roses,
Dance along the distance
weaving o'er the hills,
Beckoning the dull streets with
stray smiles wanton,
Strung with purpled roses that
the stray dawn chills.

Here now they meet tiptoe on
the corner,
Kiss behind the silence of the
curtained dark;
Then half unwilling run between
the houses,
Tracing through the pattern that
the dim lamps mark.

Steps break steps and murmur
into running,
Death upon the corner spills the
edge of dawn
Dull the torches waver and the
streets stand breathless;
Silent fades the marching and
the night-noon's gone.

Our April Letter

This is April again. Roller
skates rain slowly down the
street.
Your voice far away on the
phone.
Once I would have jumped
like a clown through a
hoop—but.
"Then the area of infection
has increased? ... Oh ...
What can I expect after all—
I've had worse shocks,
anyhow, I know and that's
something." (Like hell it is,
but it's what you say to an
X-ray doctor.)
Then the past whispering
faint now on another
phone:
"Is there any change?"

"Little or no change."
"I see."

The roller skates rain down
the streets,
The black cars shine
between the leaves,
Your voice far away:
"I am going with my
daughter to the country. My
husband left today... No he
knows nothing."
"Good."
I have asked a lot of my
emotions—one hundred
and twenty stories. The
price was high, right up with
Kipling, because there was
one little drop of
something—not blood, not
a tear, not my seed, but me
more intimately than these,

in every story, it was the extra I had. Now it has gone and I am just like you now. Once the phial was full— here is the bottle it came in.
Hold on, there's a drop left there … No, it was just the way the light fell.
But your voice on the telephone. If I hadn't abused words so, what you said might have meant something. But one hundred and twenty stories…
April evening spreads over everything, the purple blur left by a child who has used the whole paint-box.

City Dusk

COME out . . . . out
To this inevitable night of mine
Oh you drinker of new wine,
Here's pageantry . . . . Here's
carnival,
Rich dusk, dim streets and all
The whispering of city night . . .

.

I have closed my book of fading
harmonies,
(The shadows fell across me in
the park)
And my soul was sad with
violins and trees,
And I was sick for dark,
When suddenly it hastened by
me, bringing
Thousands of lights, a haunting
breeze,
And a night of streets and
singing . . . .

I shall know you by your eager
feet
And by your pale, pale hair;
I'll whisper happy incoherent
things
While I'm waiting for you there .

. . .

All the faces unforgettable in
dusk
Will blend to yours,
And the footsteps like a
thousand overtures
Will blend to yours,
And there will be more
drunkenness than wine
In the softness of your eyes on
mine . . . .

Faint violins where lovely ladies
dine,
The brushing of skirts, the
voices of the night
And all the lure of friendly eyes .
. . . Ah there
We'll drift like summer sounds
upon the summer air . . . .

One Southern Girl

Lolling down on the edge of time

Where the flower months fade as the days move over,

Days that are long like lazy rhyme,

Nights that are pale with the moon and the clover,

Summer there is a dream of summer

Rich with dusks for a lover's food –

Who is the harlequin, who is the mummer,

You or time or the multitude?

Still does your hair's gold light
the ground

And dazzle the blind till their old
ghosts rise?

Then, all you care to find being
found,

Are you yet kind to their hungry
eyes?

Part of a song, a remembered
glory –

Say there's one rose that lives
and might

Whisper the fragments of our
story:

Kisses, a lazy street – and night.

To Boath

There was a flutter from the
wings of God and you lay dead.

Your books were in your desk I
guess and some unfinished
chaos in your head

Was dumped to nothing by the
great janitress of destinies.

The Pope At Confession

The gorgeous Vatican was
steeped in night,

The organs trembled on my
heart no more,

But with a blend of colours on
my sight

I loitered through a sombre
corridor;

When suddenly I heard behind a screen

The faintest whisper as from one in prayer;

I glanced about, then passed, for I had seen

A hushed, dim-lighted room – and two were there.

A ragged friar, half in dream's
embrace,

Leaned sideways, soul intent, as
if to seize

The last grey ice of sin that
ached to melt

And faltered from the lips of
him who knelt,

A little bent old man upon his
knees

With pain and sorrow in his holy
face.

Above: Francis Scott Fitzgerald's
Signature

Francis Scott Fitzgerald (1896 - 1940)

Photograph appearing in "The World's Work" (1921)

End

Connect with the author

www.debbiebrewer.co.uk

https://www.facebook.com/DebbieBrewerPoetry

www.instagram.com/poetrytreasures

www.twitter.com/poetrytreasure

www.ingramcontent.com/pod-product-compliance
Lightning Source LLC
Chambersburg PA
CBHW061458040426
42450CB00008B/1413